The purpose of this publication is not to glamorize narcotics or illicit drug use,
but to present the history of a subculture through the artifacts and essays within.

We at Blurring Books feel moved by the Japanese concept known as 'mono no aware',
which translates to 'a sensitivity to ephemera'. The ephemera documented in this book
are artifacts of a time in our shared history and offer commentary on consumer culture.

Perhaps the most outrageous set of crossed signals between the drug underground and the hegemonic culture of seduction and control has been in the curious history of heroin bag branding in New York City. Put into small glassine envelopes that are folded over and taped shut, the identity of each seller and copping spot is designated by the marking of each bag with an inked rubber stamp. A common practice for decades now, it remains absolutely necessary for users needing to distinguish between the extremely erratic quality levels of the various street level distribution networks. The roster of names and pictures over the years may connote a junkie mythology for a very few but has by and large existed under the radar of mainstream attention. Collections have been made, many rumored to still exist, but as a kind of passionate obsession that most often leads to either getting clean or dying, it is hard to imagine a single long-term archive. What we do know however, is that in its most common forms of impersonation, heroin bag branding has simultaneously celebrated itself as both a bogus currency of glamour and a nihilistic stigma of the grotesque. Among the former we see a ghetto vernacular that is proto-bling-bling to the point of absurdity, with brands bearing such inappropriate names as Dom Perignon and Executive. Conversely however, heroin consumption has equally embraced its most vilified of terms, with very successful brand names including the likes of Toilet and Poison.

Rather lowly as an aesthetic discipline, the medium of heroin bag branding has been dictated by the accessibility and ease of rubber stamps. Thus the only real form of innovation has been of the kind of radical minimalist word art previously cited- which was as simple to create as going to a local stationary store for a customized rubber stamp. It is however, worth mentioning that much of the stamps have been chosen from the pre-made, mass-manufactured items offering a proliferation of comic art insignias from the Smurfs to Spiderman.

-From the 2003 article "High Art" by Carlo McComick

Branded Bronx Bags

Death, Sex and Trouble
The Marketing of Street Drugs
1984-1994

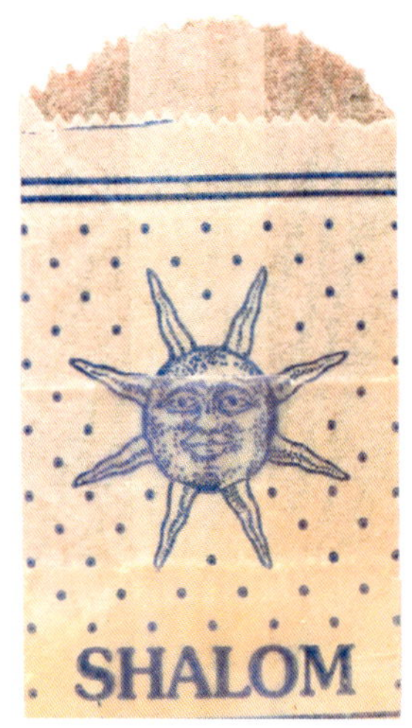

Actual Size

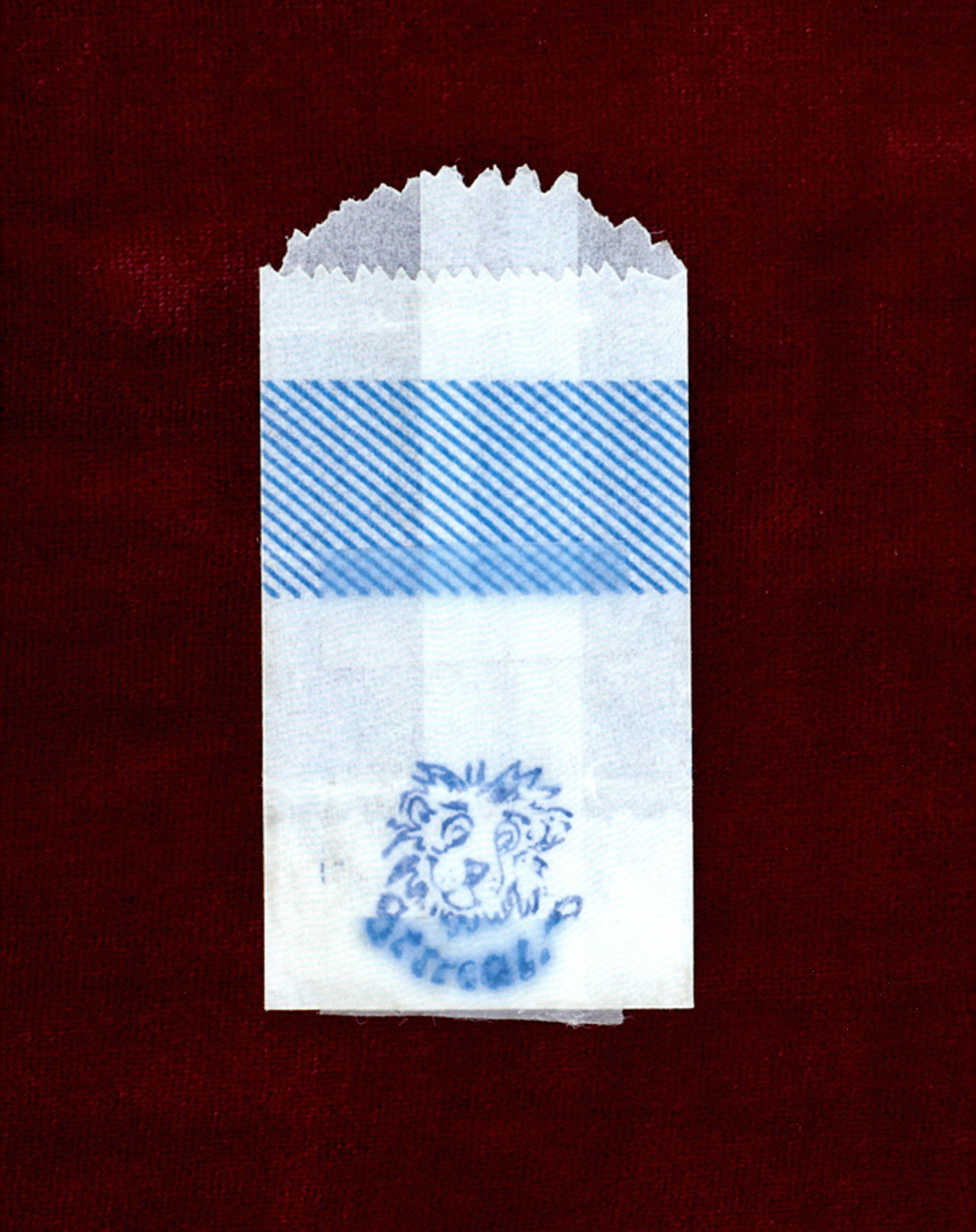

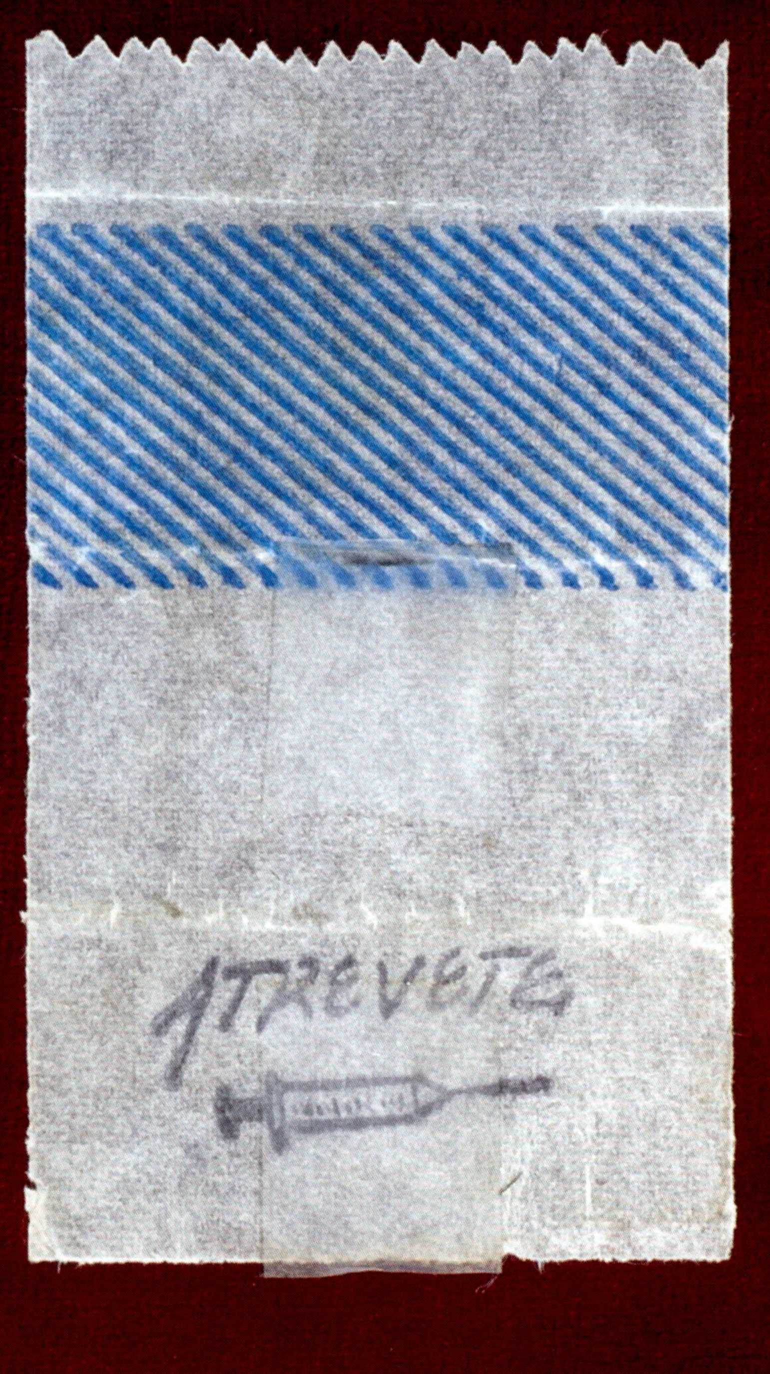
ATREVETE

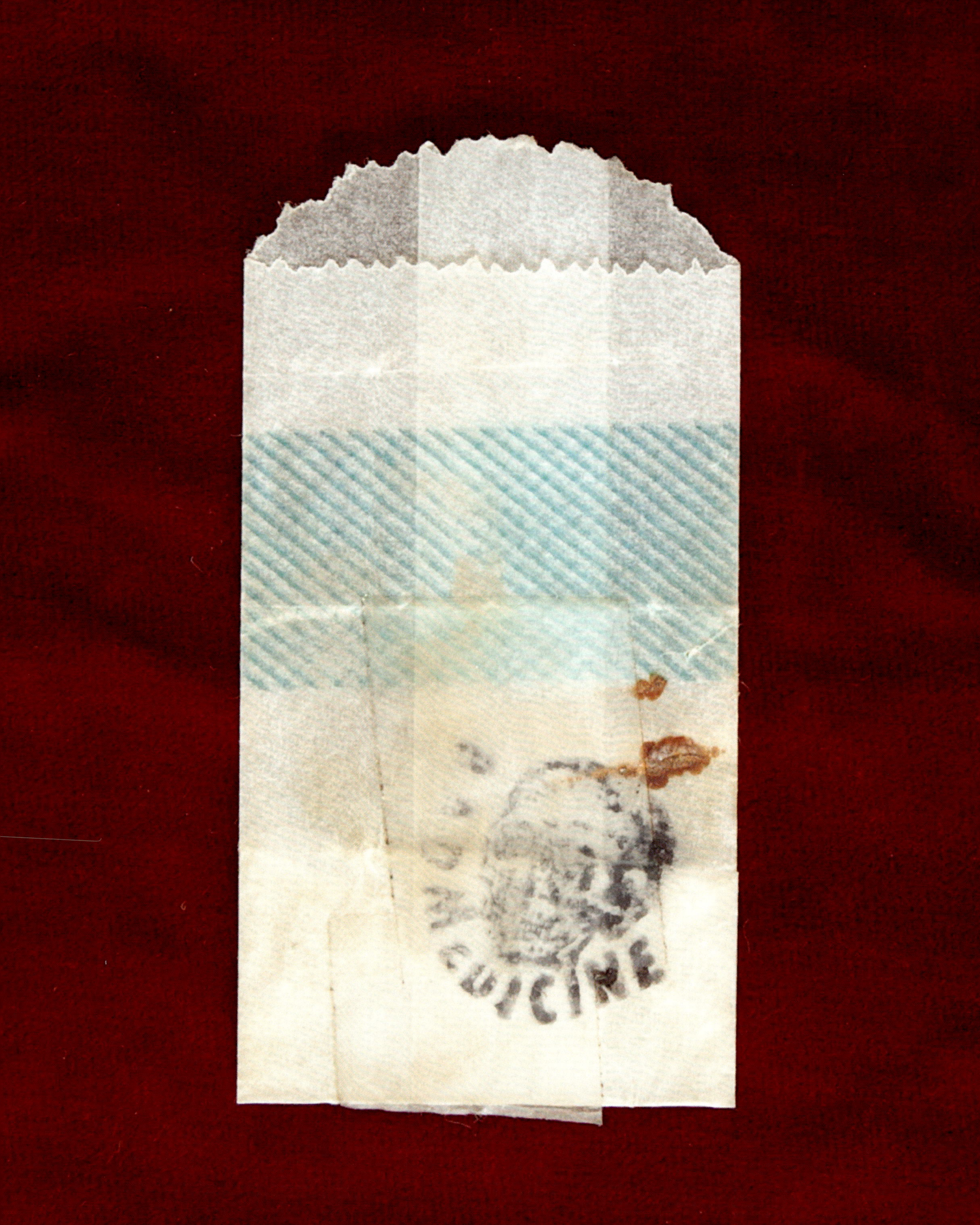
MEDICINE

EXPLOTION
MIKE TYZON
BABILON
MISHELIN

ANDREW
CINDY

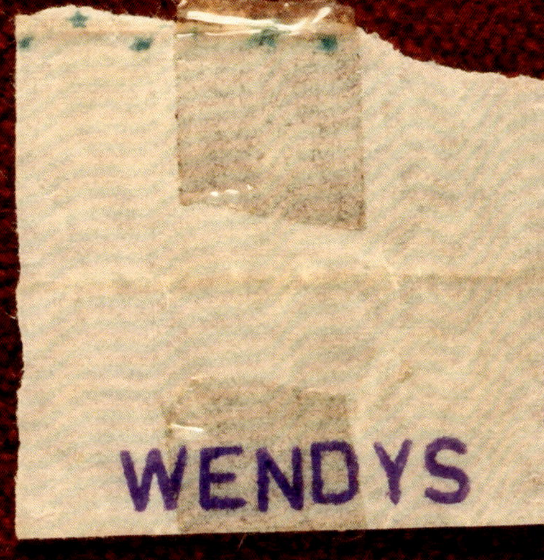

WENDYS

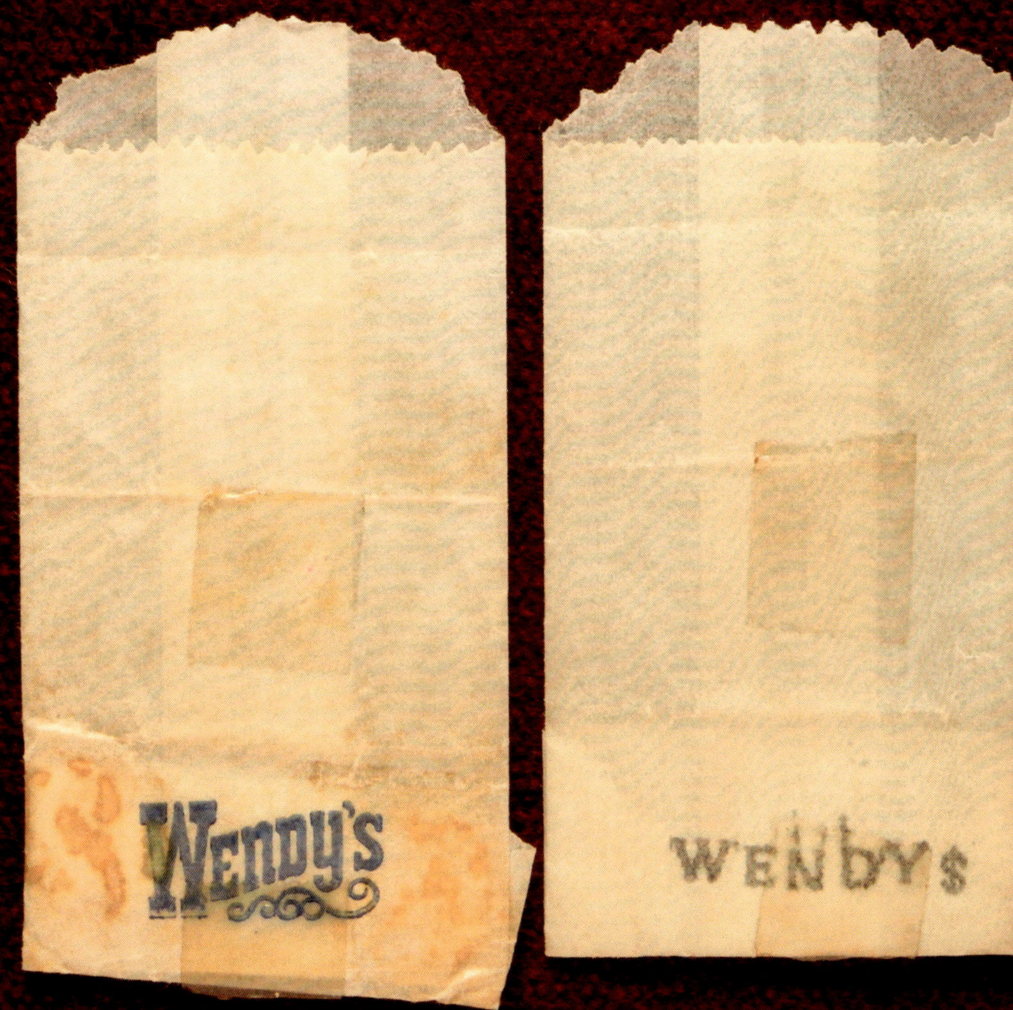

Wendy's
WENDYS

HIT & RUN

Poseidón

BATMAN

UNTOUCHABLES

MONTANA

KNOCKOUT

Respect

LEGEND

STORM

POWER

HOMICIDE

DRAGON

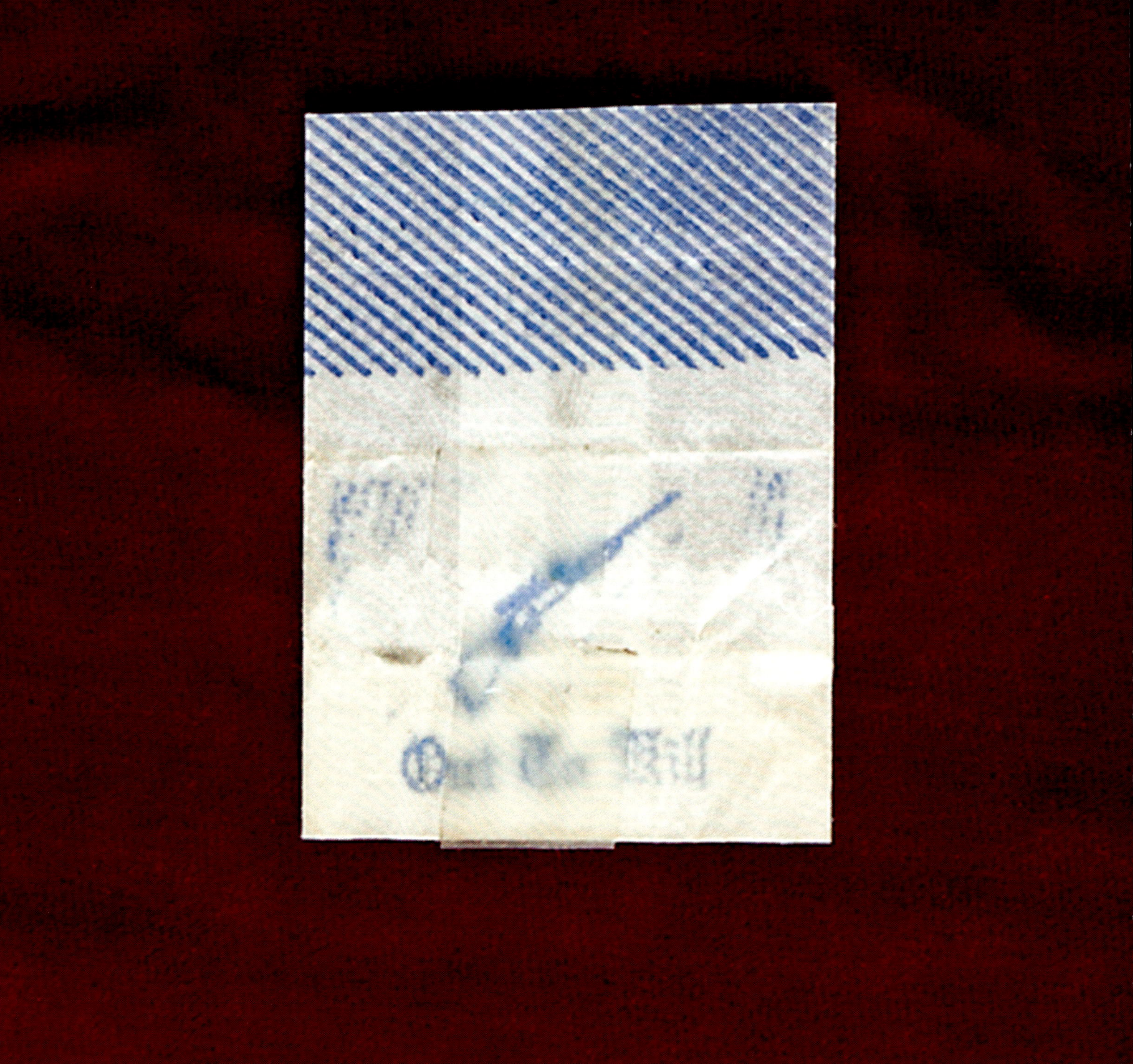

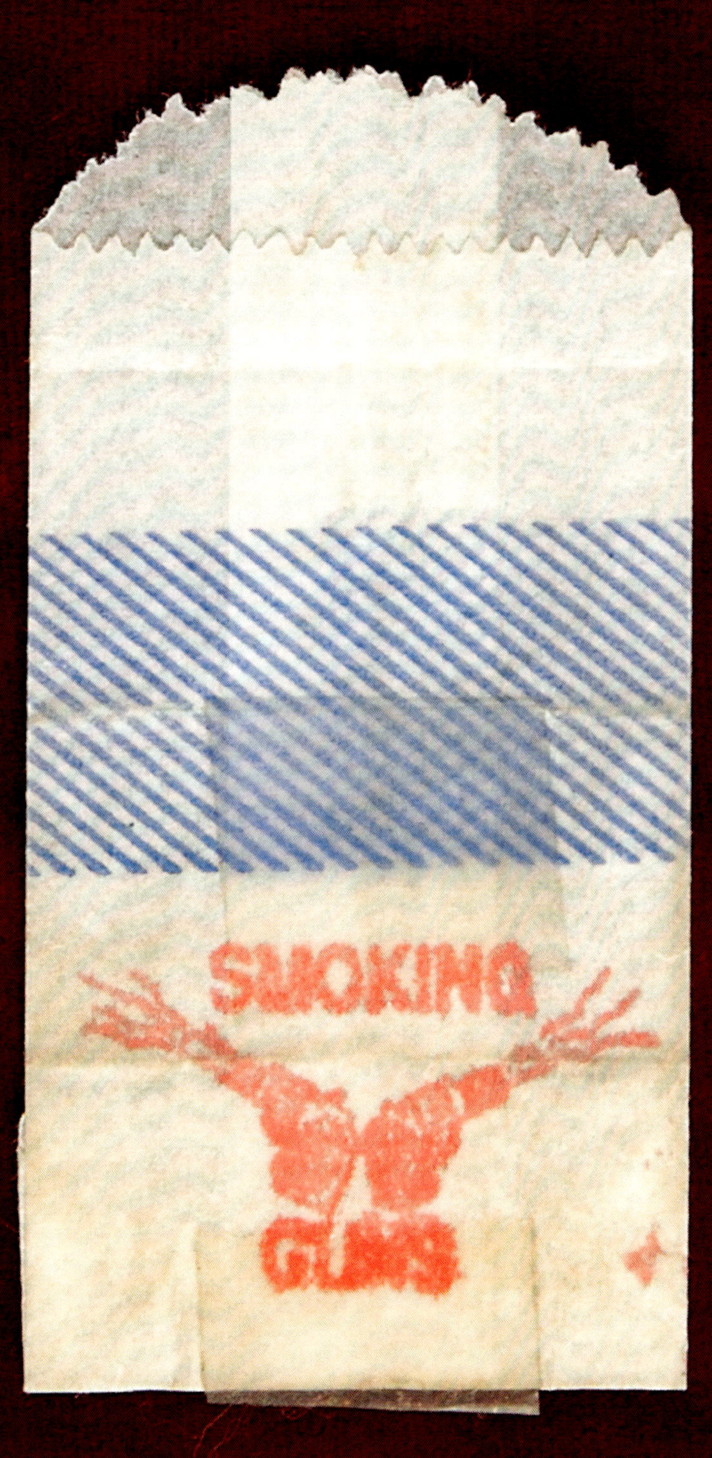
SMOKING
GUNS

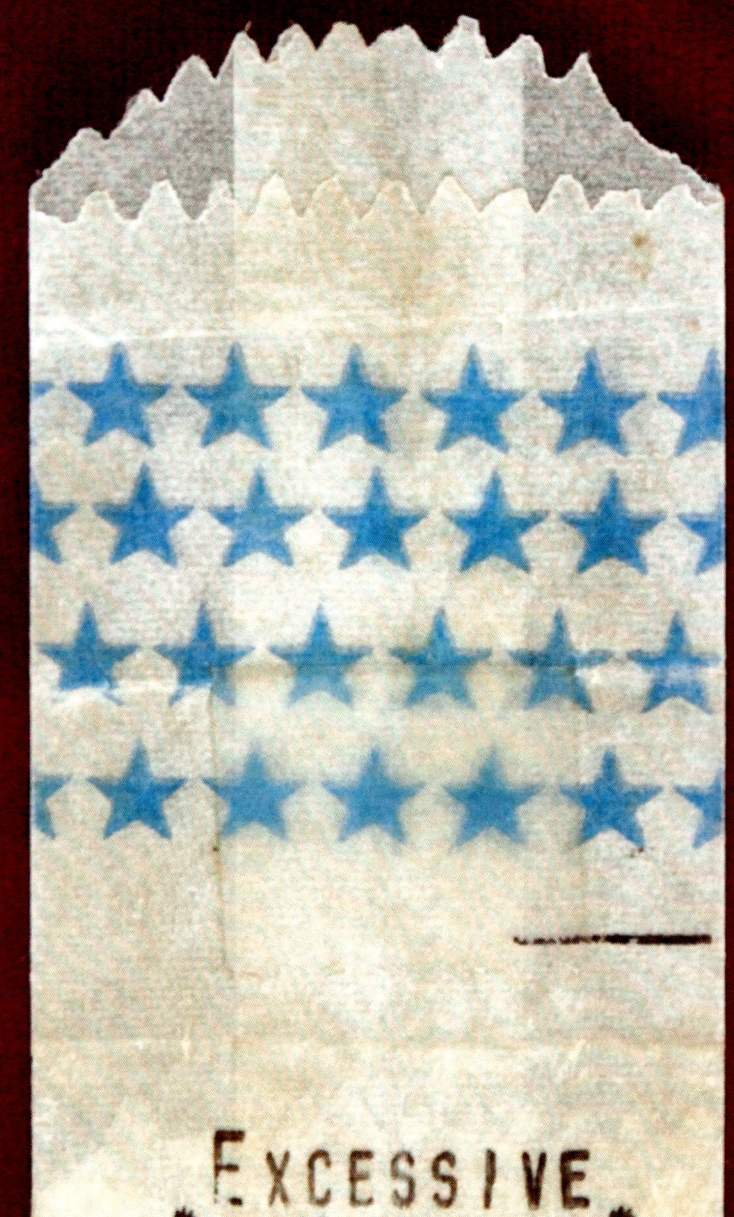

EXCESSIVE
FORCE

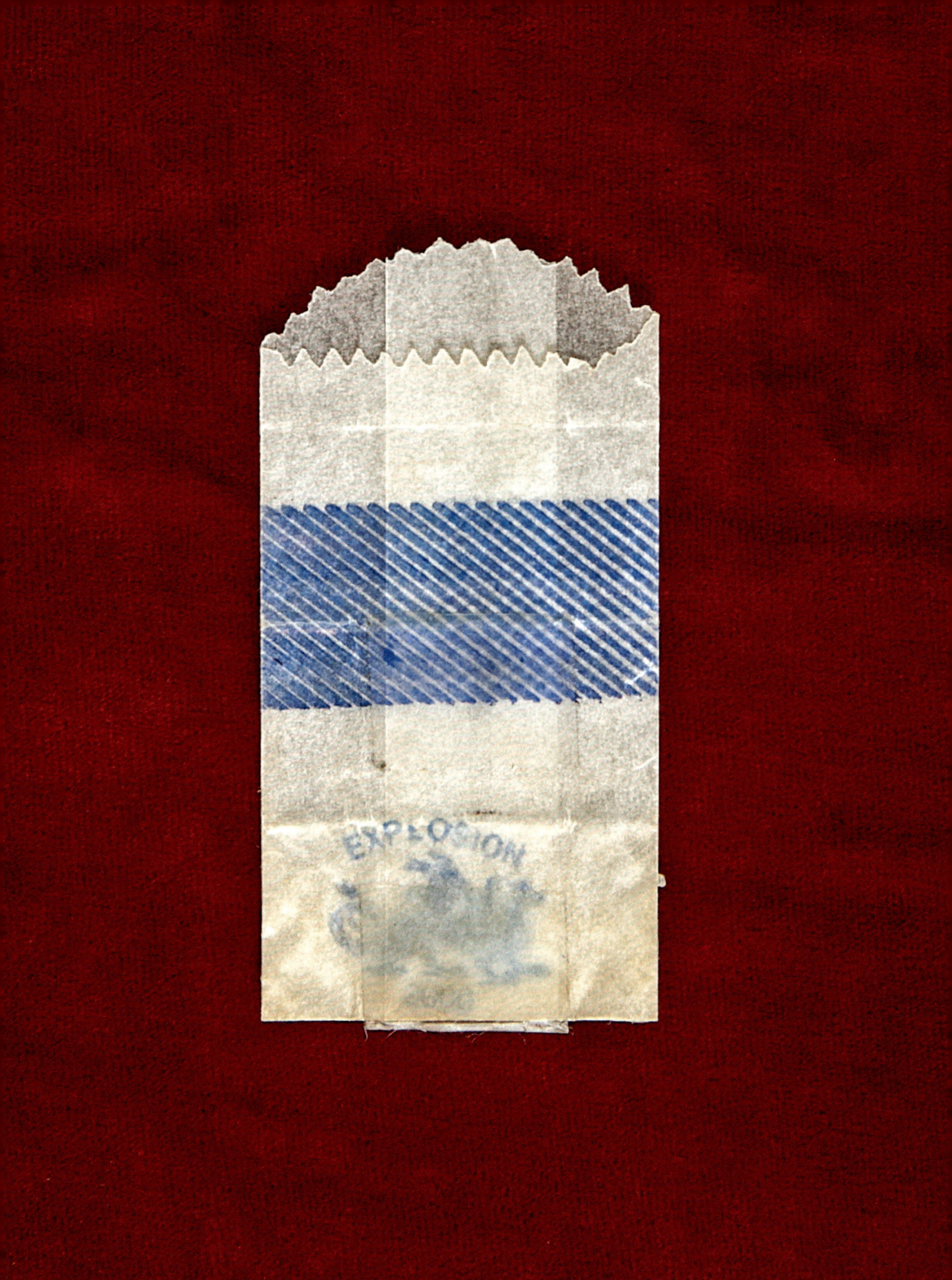
EXPLOSION

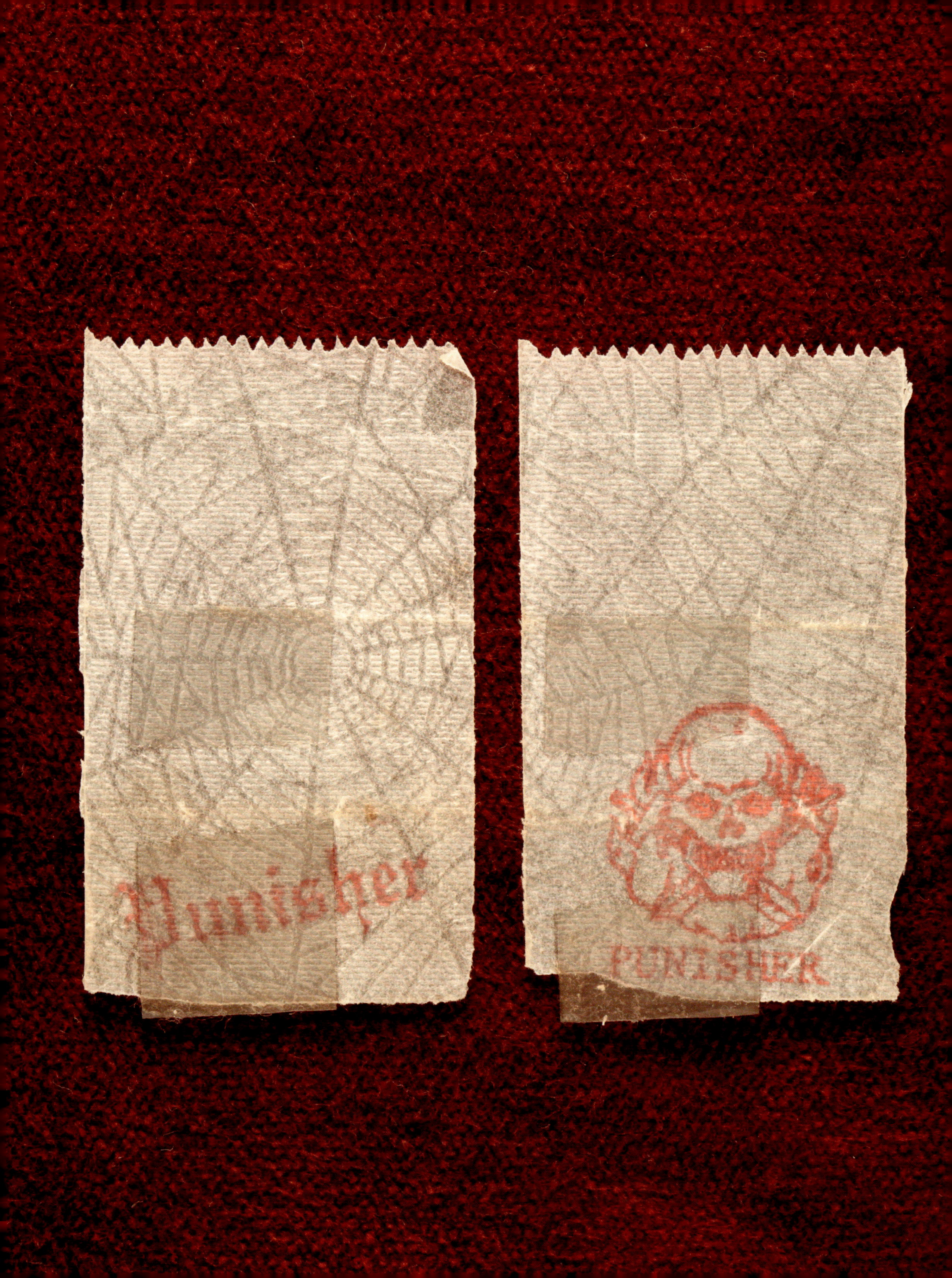
Punisher
PUNISHER

ARMED AND
DANGEROUS

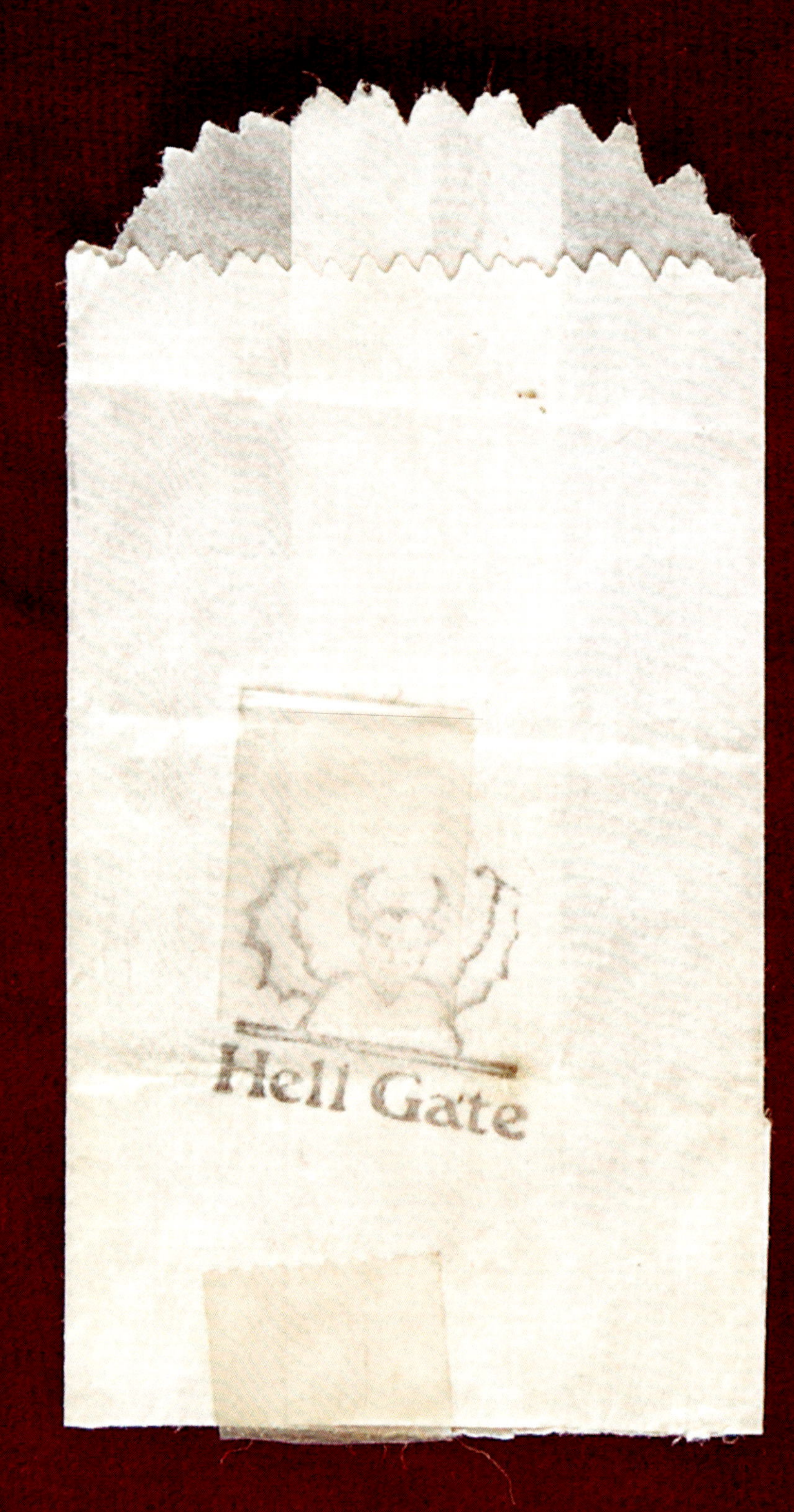

Hell Gate

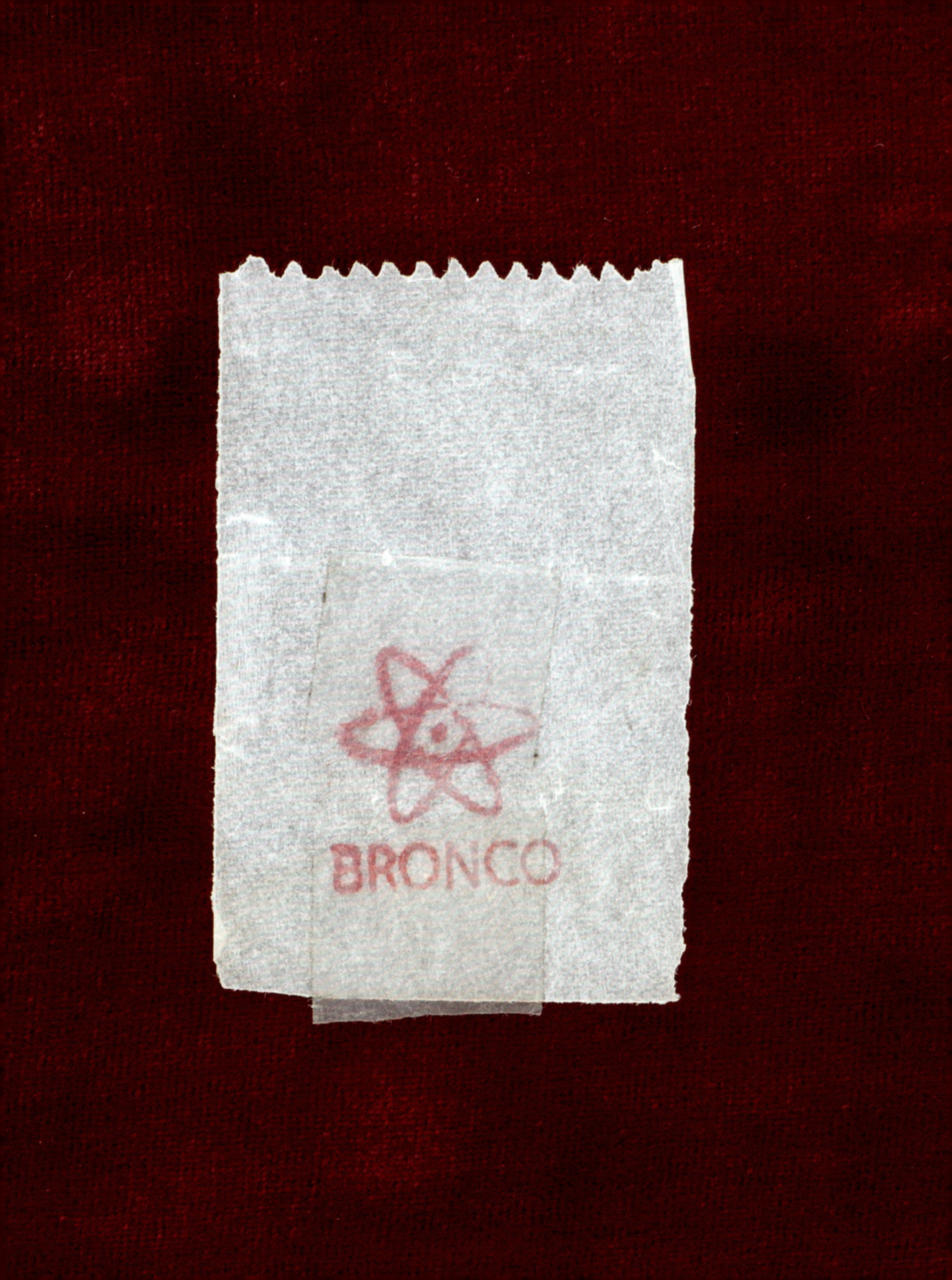

BRONCO

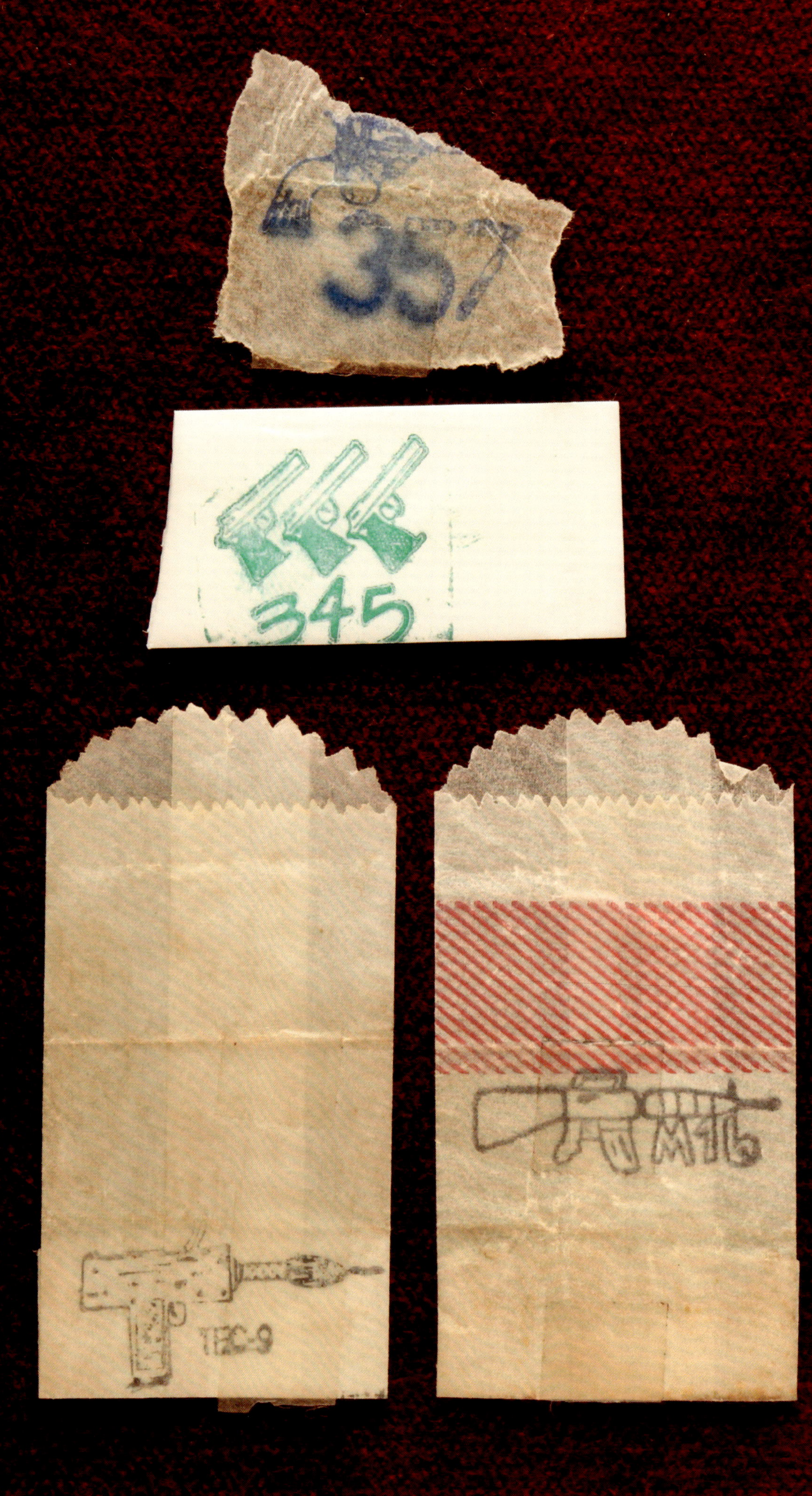
357
345
TEC-9
M16

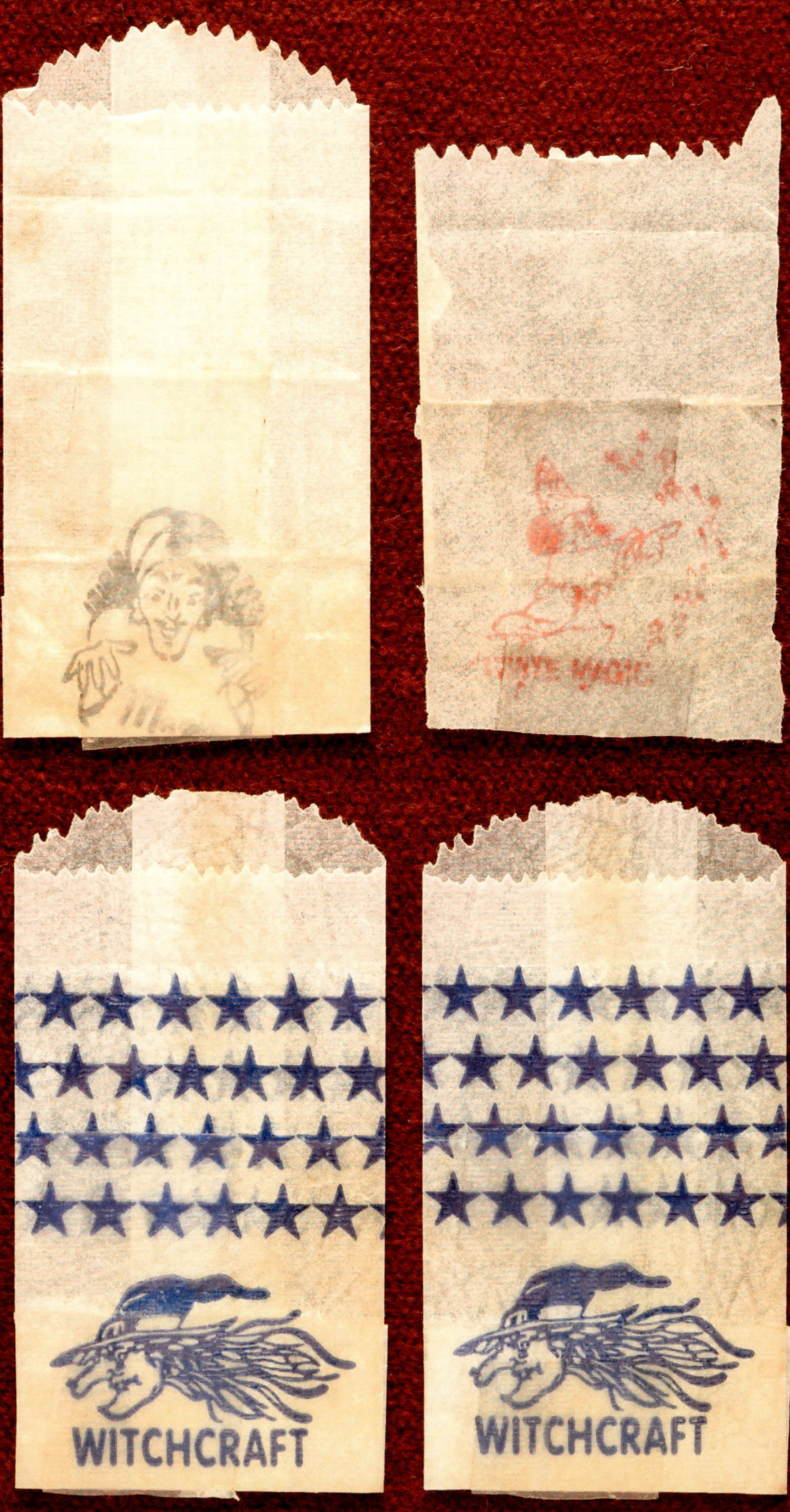
WITCHCRAFT
WITCHCRAFT

BE ON TIME

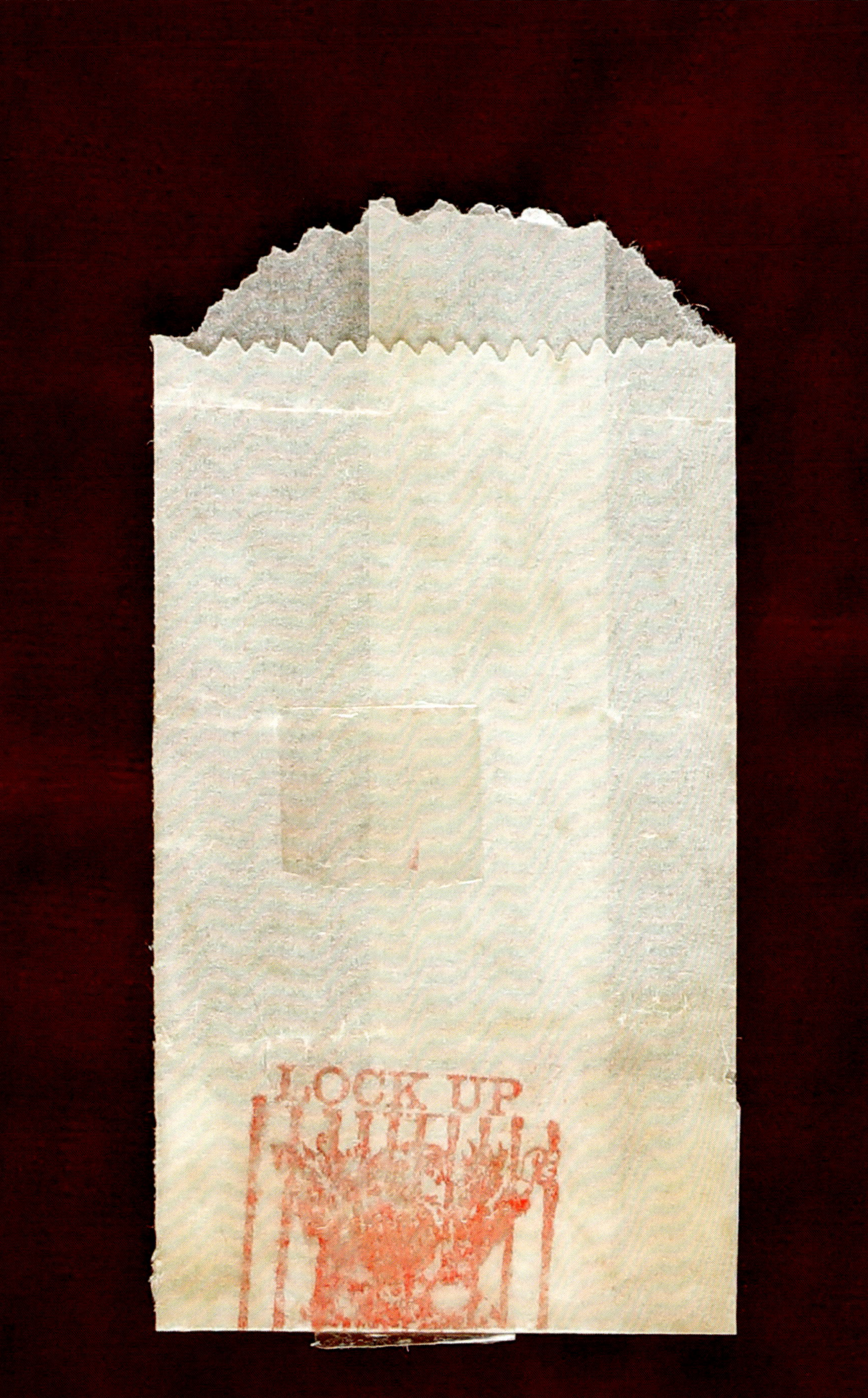

LOCK UP

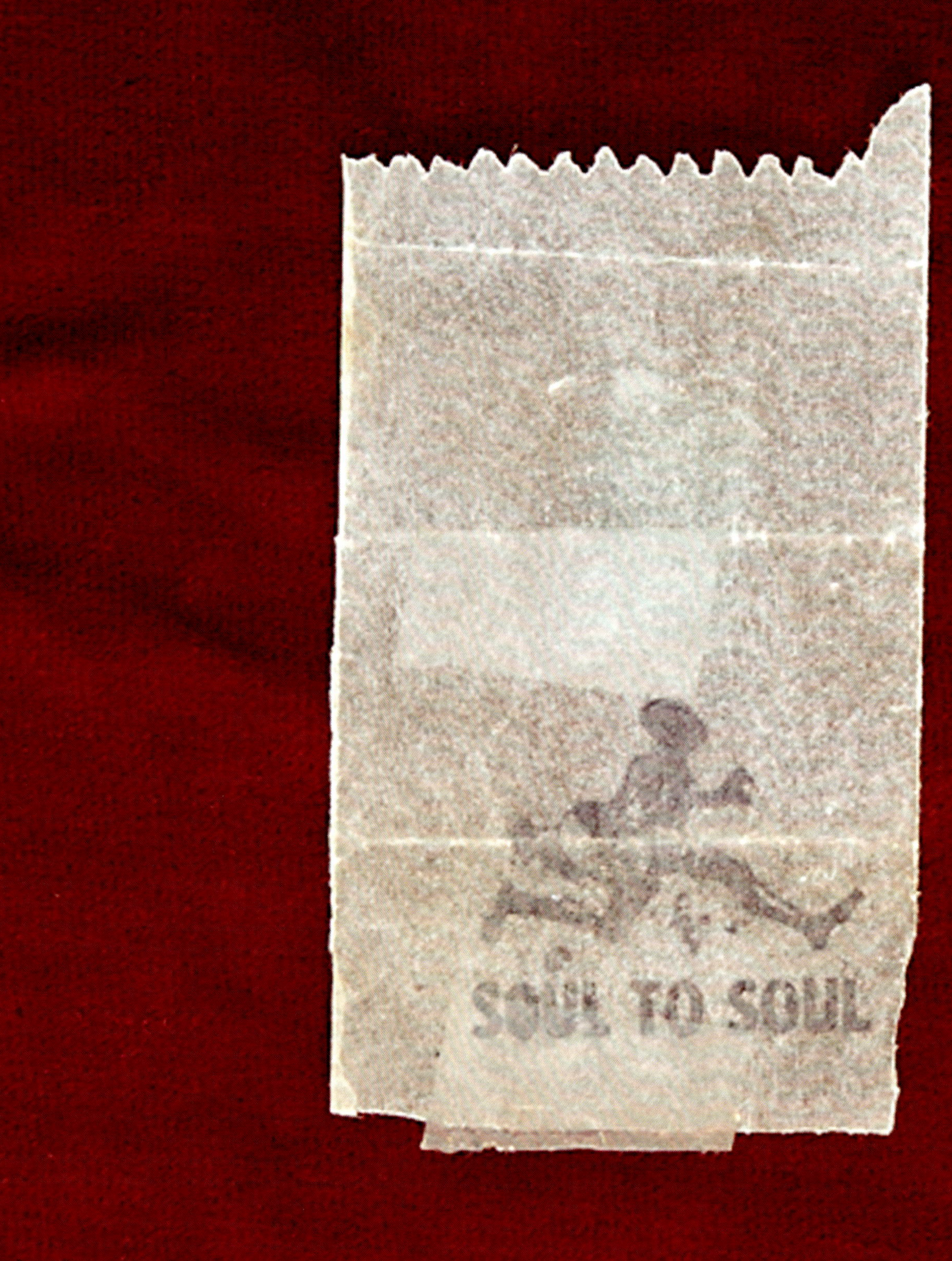
SOUL TO SOUL

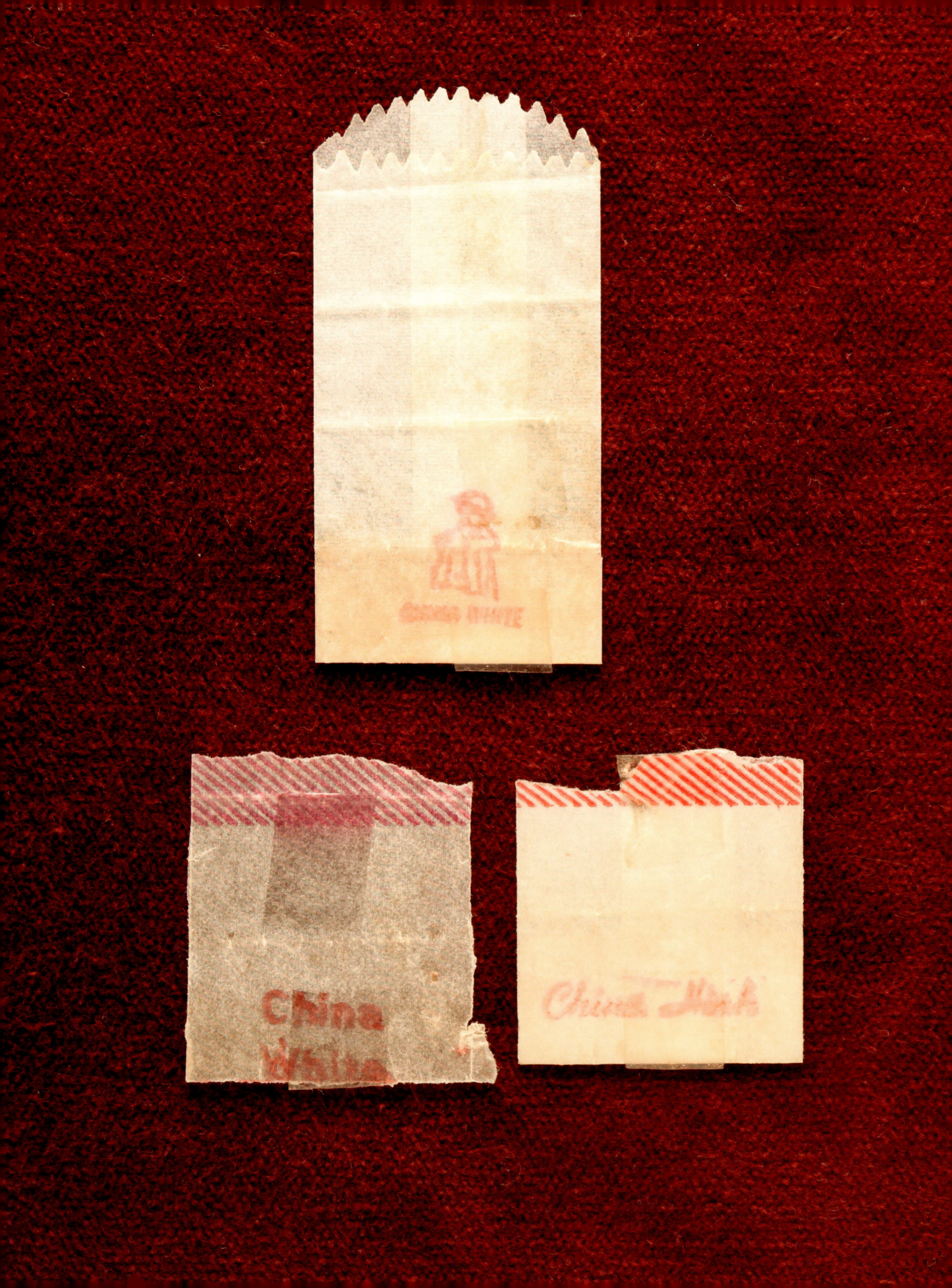

CHINA WHITE
China
White
China White

NEW JACK CITY

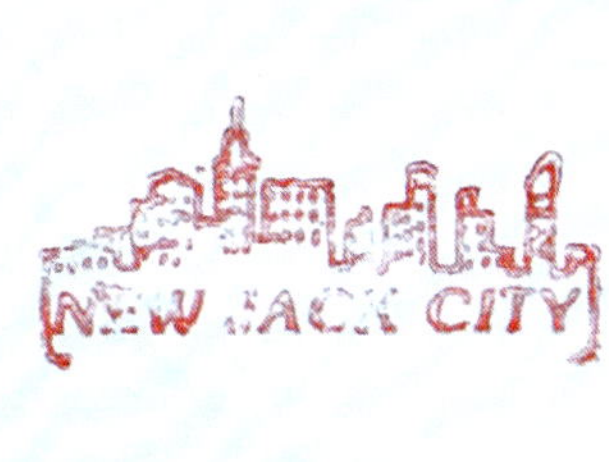
NEW JACK CITY

NEW JACK CITY

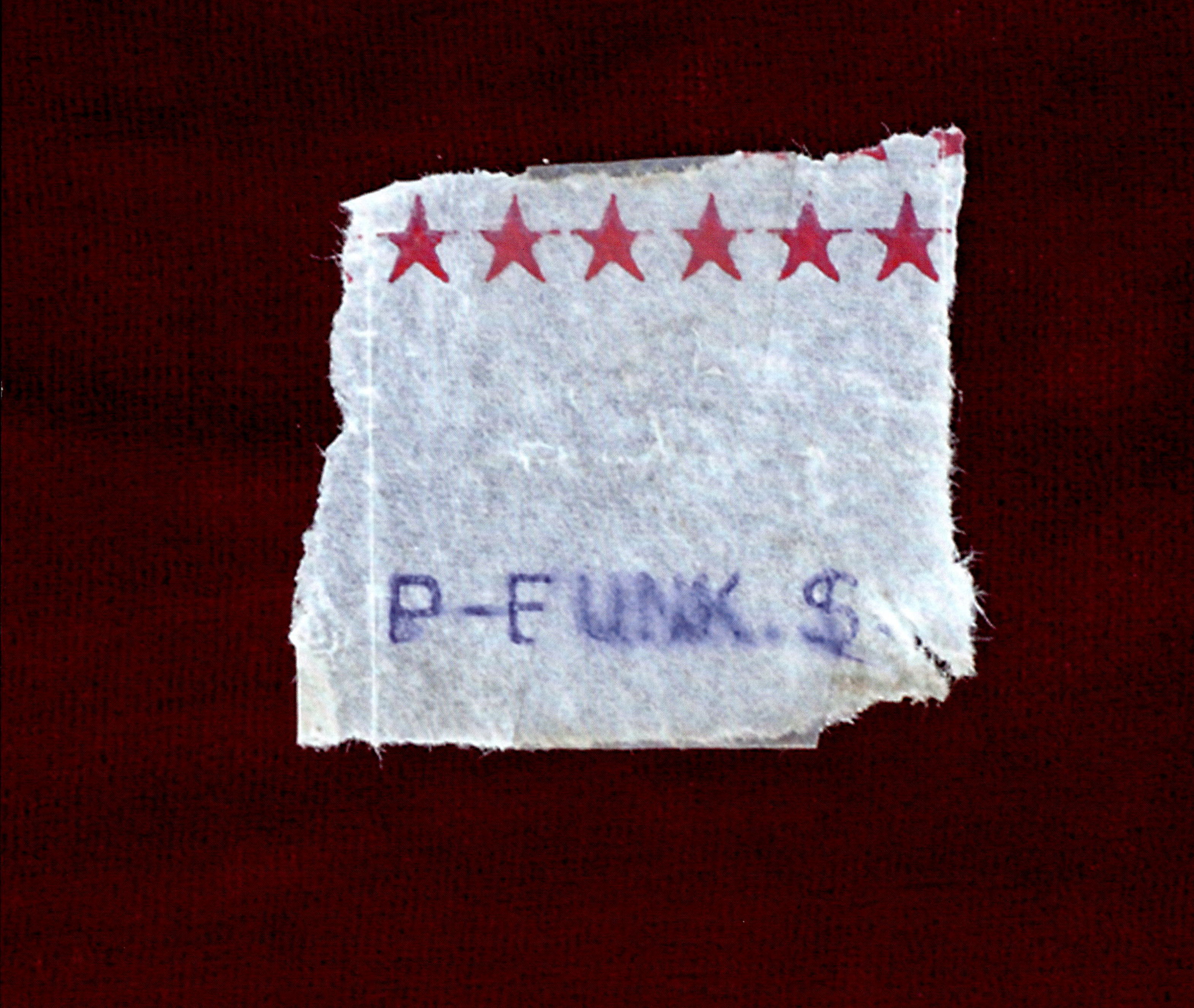
P-FUNK.S.

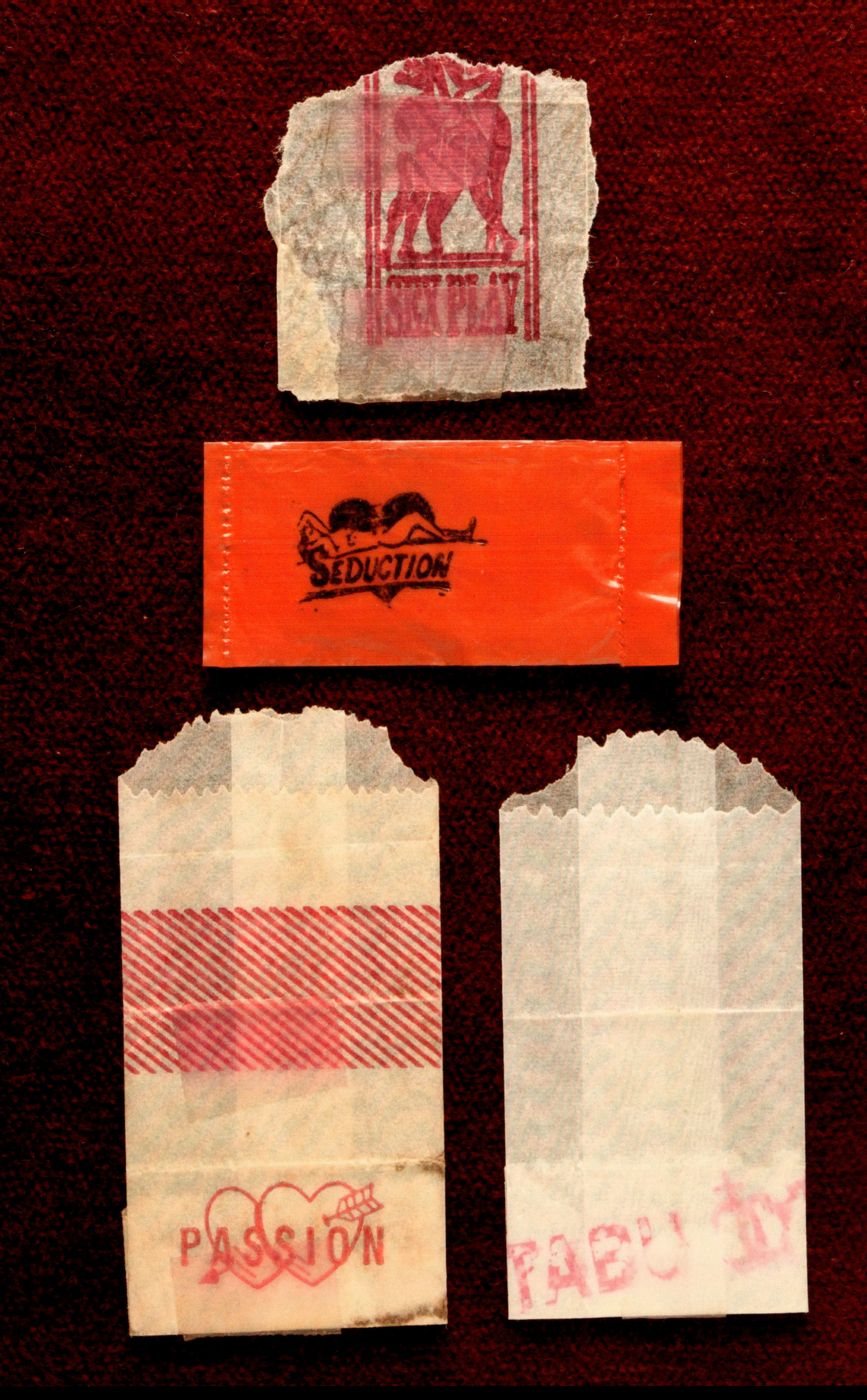
SEX PLAY
SEDUCTION
PASSION
FABU

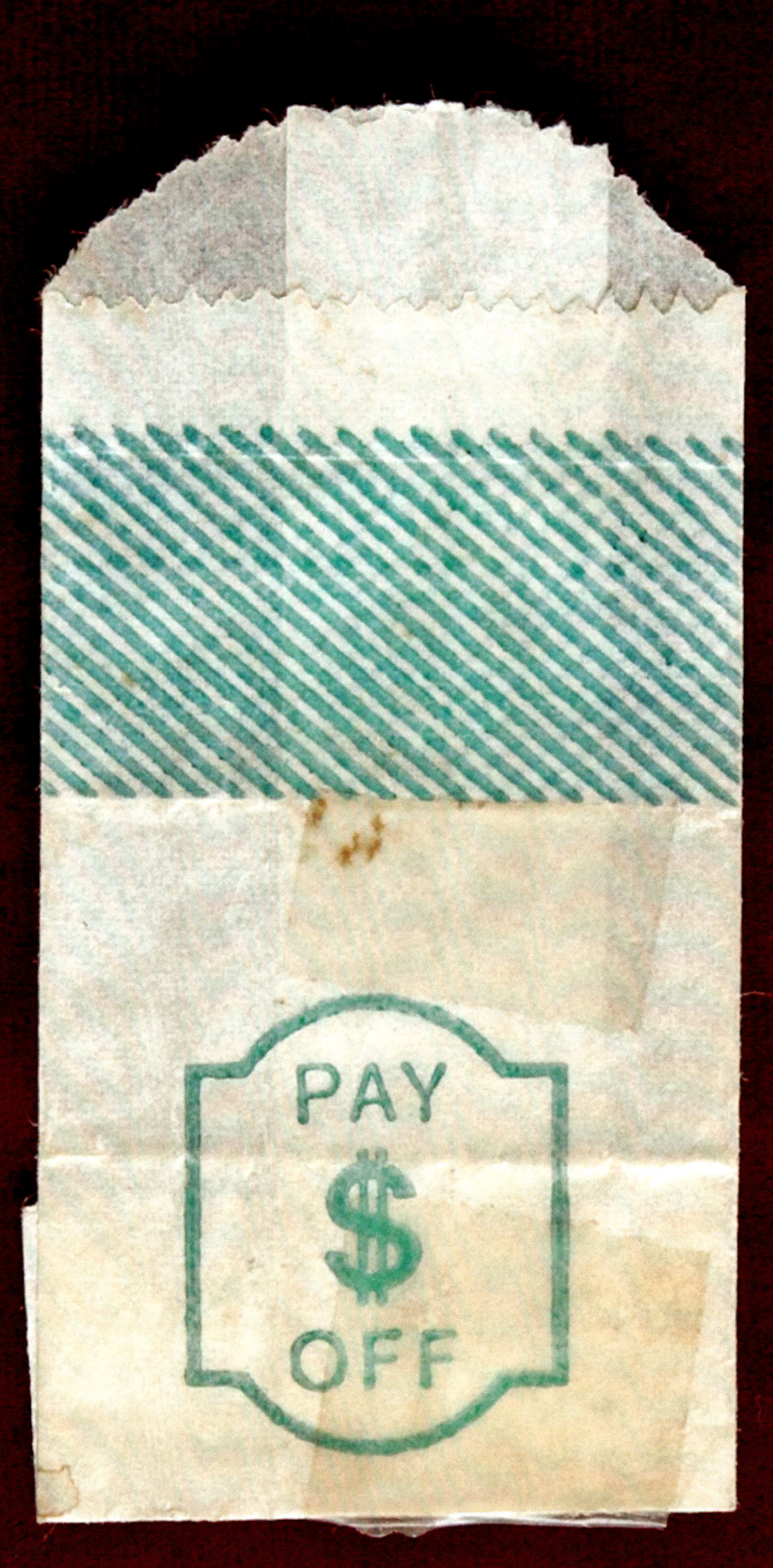

PAY
$
OFF

SKELETON

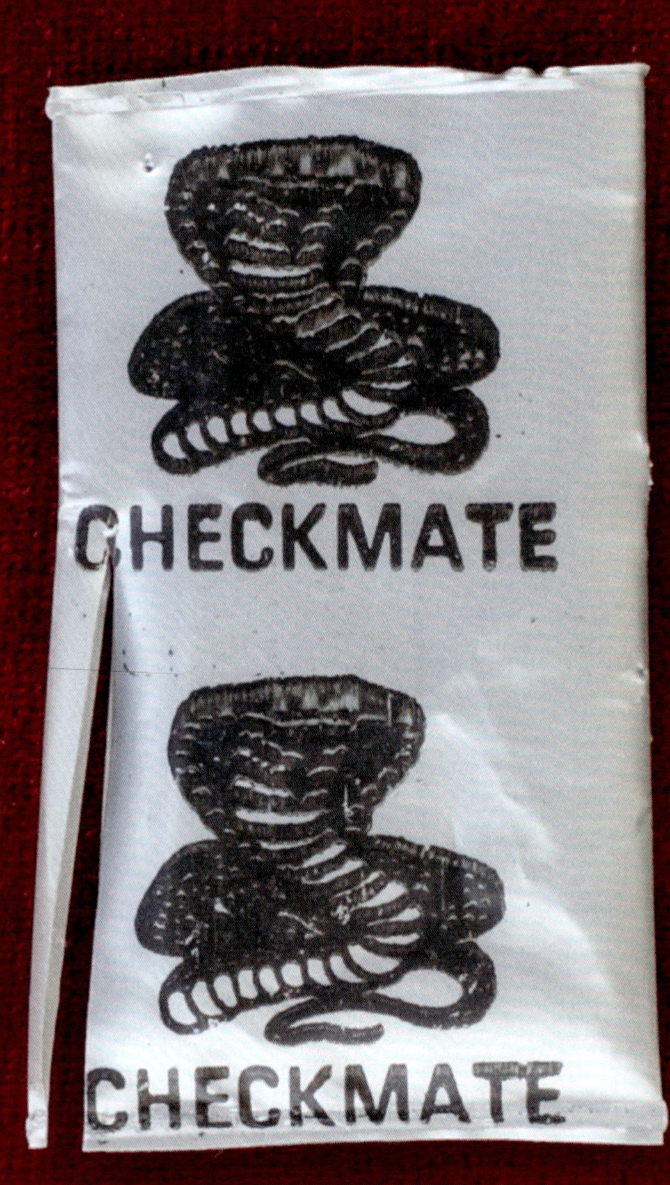

CHECKMATE
CHECKMATE

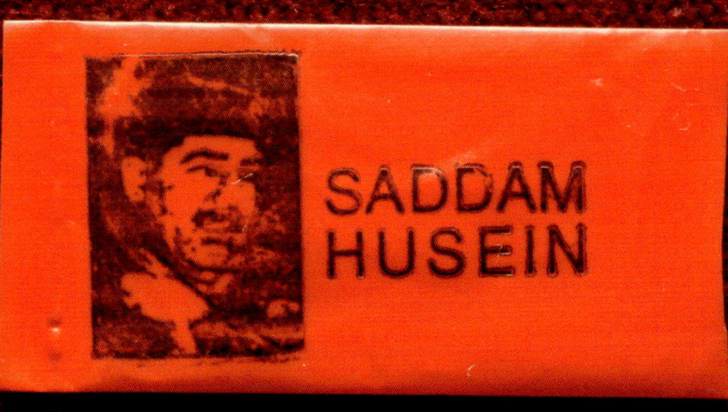

SADDAM
HUSEIN

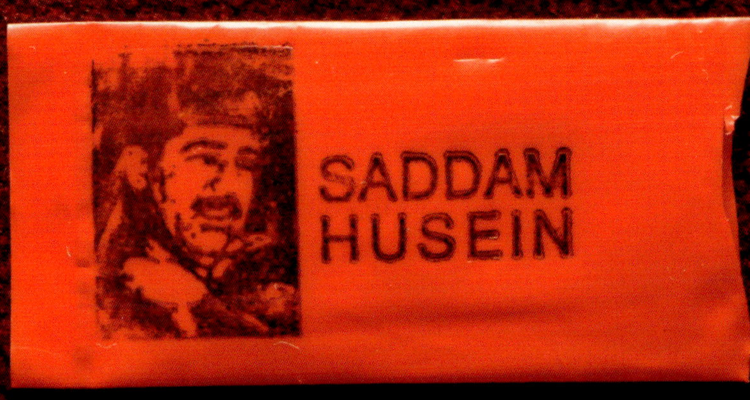

SADDAM
HUSEIN

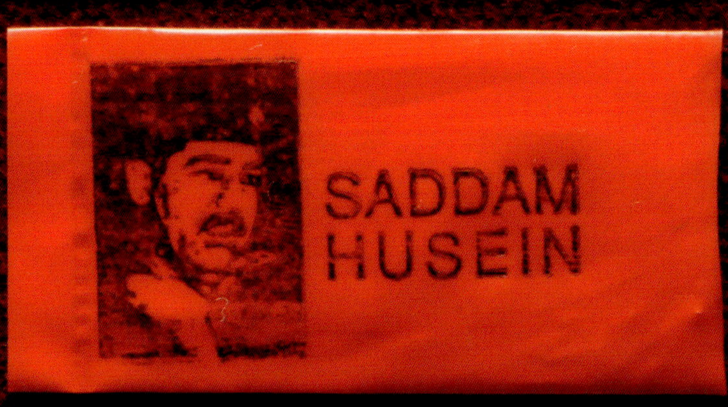

SADDAM
HUSEIN

JUDGEMENT DAY

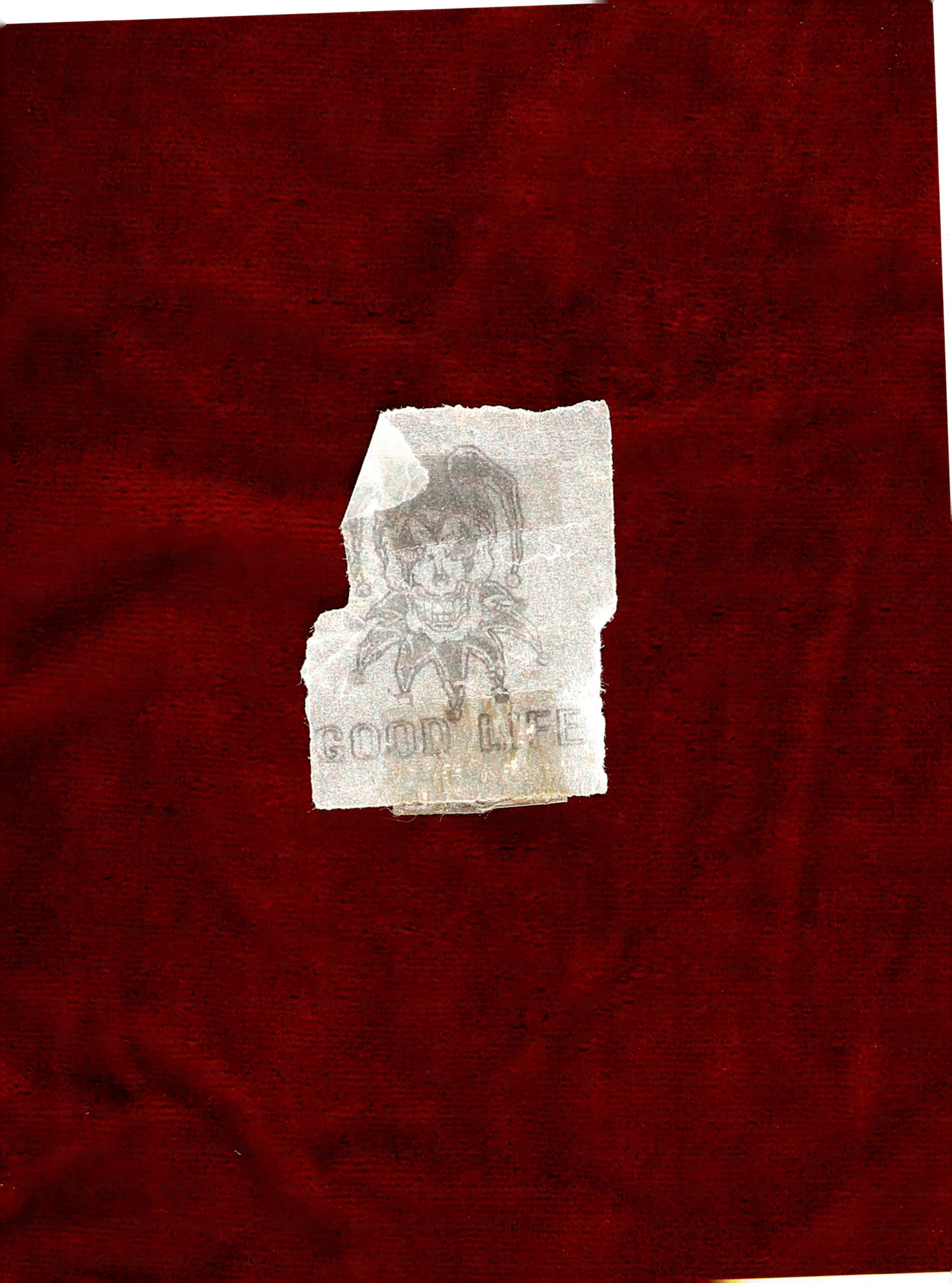

GOOD LIFE

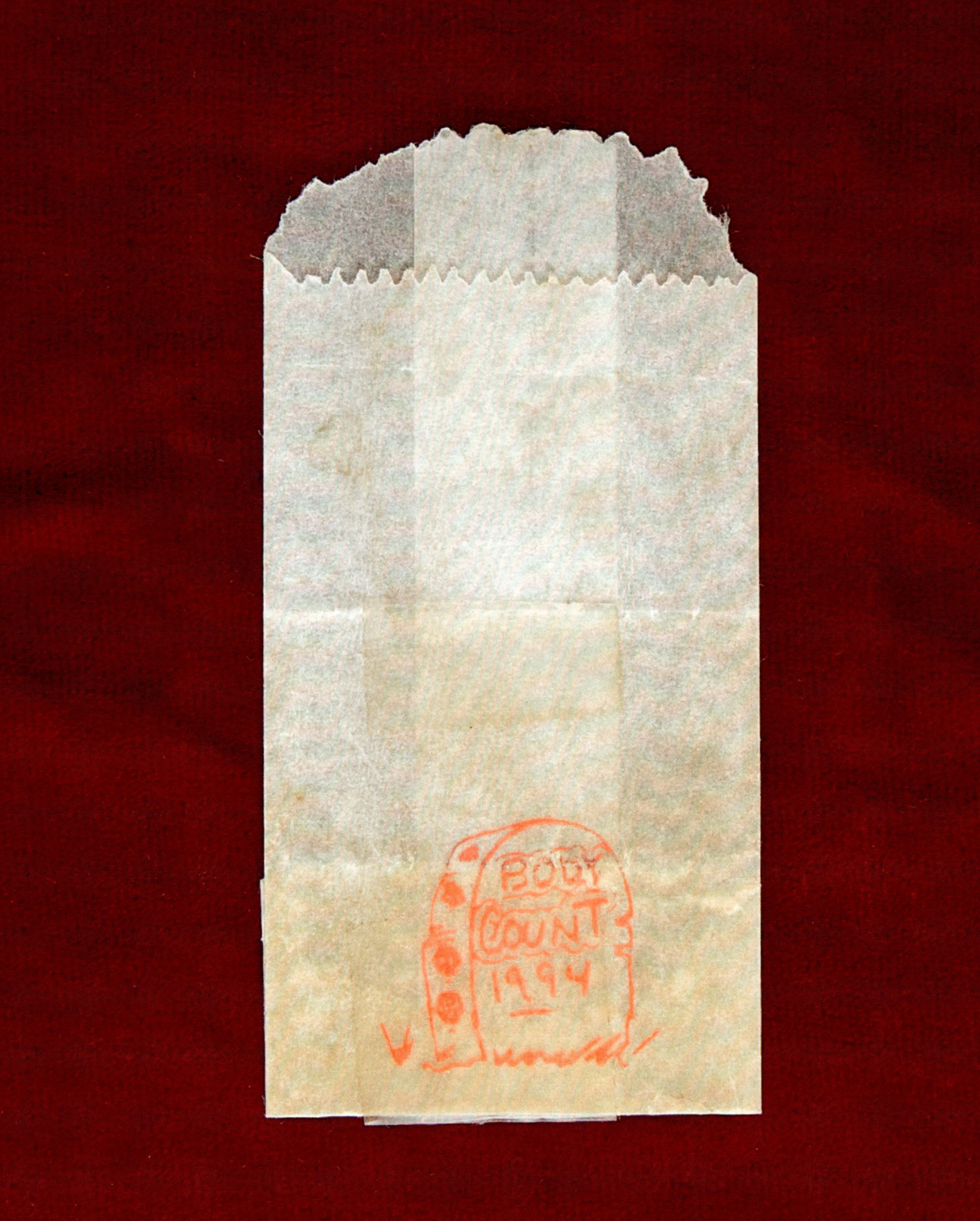
BODY
COUNT
1994

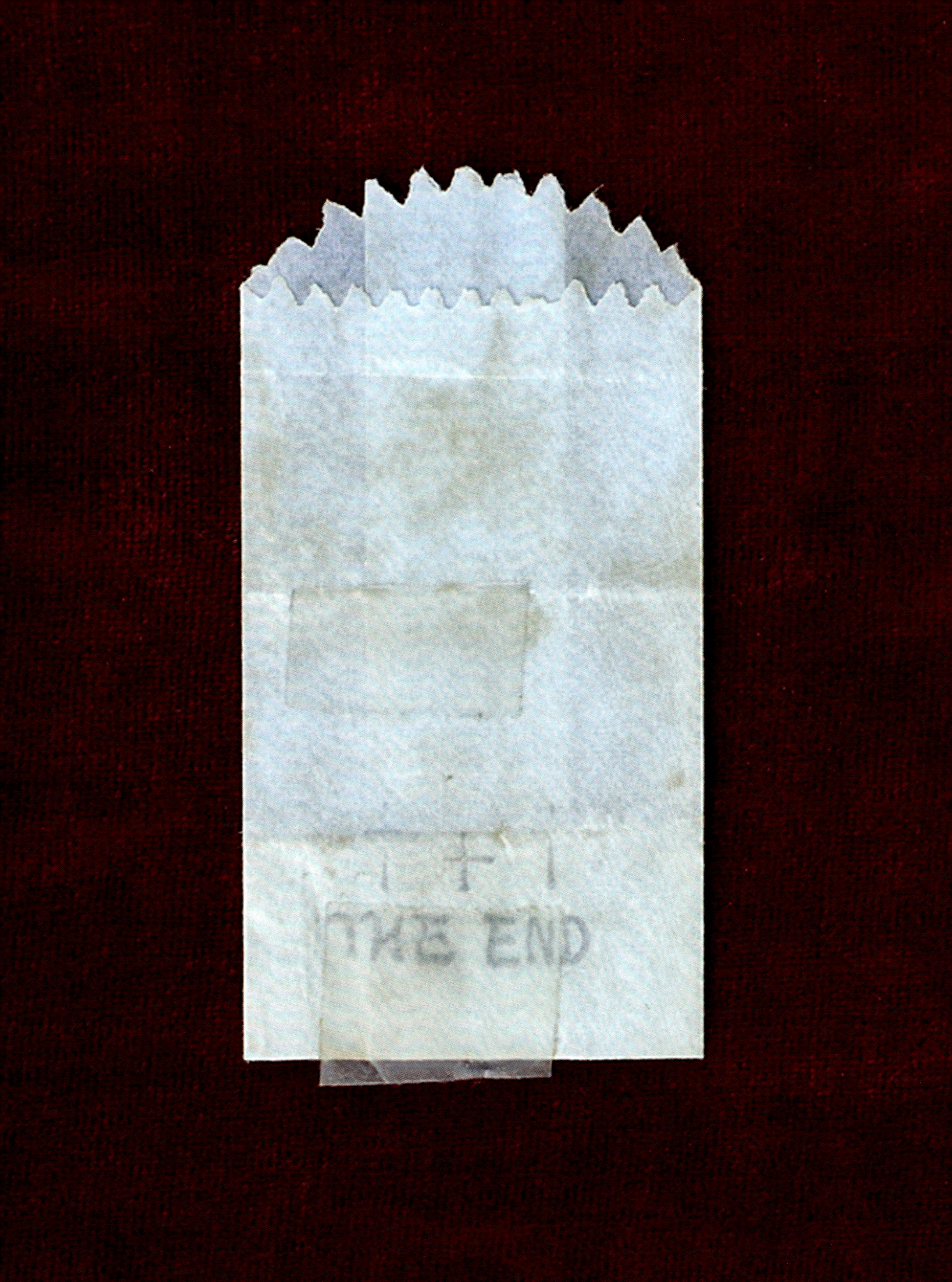

THE END

I got to The Bronx in 1984 in the years of crack, AIDS and box cutters. My father, who had been born there, said "That's great that you got a nice apartment but aren't you taking your life into your own goddamn hands Thatcher?" I arrived to a post apocalyptic landscape: kind of like Mad Max except people were after drugs, not gasoline. In the mid 80's the trains were still thick with the hieroglyphic gibberish of graffiti. My borough savvy girlfriend laid out for me that these scrawlings were the territorial signatures of local (largely) unschooled artists aka "writers." I loved the notion of a secret language and a special club of people communicating right there under the noses of the citizenry and the commuters.

Friends who worked social medicine jobs explained to me some of the standards and practices of the street. The long lines of people waiting in front of burnt out abandoned shells of buildings were waiting to buy drugs. And the ridiculously dressed women and transvestites were street walking freelance prostitutes on the stroll.

Both sex and drugs were big business uptown. I saw all the empty color topped mini vials and stamp collecting bags that were everywhere. The vial tops were in different colors (crack) and the glassines (heroin and cocaine) had different names. These were the proprietary brands sold by different dealers. That enabled the users to search for the quality products by name.

One of my darkroom co-workers was a former mid-level dealer who worked the junction between the mafia and the street dealer. They had an office/factory with different "brands" that would be packaged for different "spots" or selling locations. You could often deduce bags that came from the same distribution point by the font or color or texturing of the bags. I learned that in The Bronx brands of heroin were labeled with names associated with death, trouble and the law. Think: Toe Tag, Body Bag, Muerte, Asesino, Don't Be Late, Overdose, Checkmate. Powder cocaine usually referenced good living and the high life such as Gucci, Love Affair and White Wedding.

I started to collect these bags. I was hanging out with the early harm reduction crew in The Bronx: epidemiologists, the Burnside needle exchange program, the psych unit at the Franklin Men's Shelter and the Hunt's Point sex worker crew that handed out condoms and bleach kits on the stroll.

It was a difficult time in The Bronx. Crack and AIDS had swept through the city, especially in the borough. At that time you could get on the 4 train in the zip code with the highest AIDS infection rate in the USA. Four stops later you were in the wealthiest zip code in the United States. Tensions were high. It was a harrowing and tragic time. Moms would roll up to the needle exchange with their children in strollers.

In 1989 I moved from an apartment near the Poe Cottage neighborhood to a Department of Cultural Affairs artist loft near Yankee Stadium in the South South Bronx. The drug detritus around 167th street was legion. I knew nice people and regular people and scary people in these years. But they were all people: human, fallible and deserving of TLC.

This would be the juncture where I would make my argument for normalization or legalization but I won't. Suffice to say if that were to happen, the collateral damage to the lives, properties, families and health from the drug economy would drop precipitously. And I say this as a victim of numerous incidents of drug related crime.

This book evidences a community of scoundrels and criminals who never the less had enormous wit, intelligence and creativity at work aside all the havoc and destruction that their drugs unleashed. Just as graffiti is vandalism it is a also bottom up creative expression of a population otherwise deprived of avenues for ambition and artistic merit. The branding of street drugs also evidences a savvy and a business sense and an advertising brilliance outside of the legitimate world. These names and images had topical references, jokes, secret messages and even poetry. It was positively Joycean.

- Thatcher Keats

The world I began using in was a world in rapid flux. Almost as soon as I mastered it, the contraption we made with a hypodermic needle, eye dropper, and baby pacifier (the one that farted air into you as it was emptied into a vein) was replaced by the single unit (disposable - but not disposed of by us) insulin syringe. The powder drugs that I'd bought in bulk, directly from the dealer's spoon to my waiting cooker began to be sold in smaller units, prepackaged in slips of paper, or in undecorated undifferentiated stamp collecting bags.

Thatcher and I met soon after I'd stopped using and took my first drug users' health job - social services coordinator for Odyssey House; an in-patient, drug free, residential therapeutic community in the Synanon House model which meant we punitively shaved heads, ran "encounter groups," gave "visual awarenesses," [i.e. sandwich boards and neck signs meant to humble and humiliate]. Odyssey House, too, was experiencing a time of rapid transition and during this time people started dying of weird things. Thatcher and I were close friends as I transitioned away from the specialty language and specific environment that was Odyssey House to a drug counselor job for a psychiatric support service run by the new graduates of a social medicine program inside an enormous men's shelter in the Franklin Armory. These were the 80s, those fraught few years when rarified smoked freebase cocaine morphed into "ready rock." What then came to be known as Crack was cheap, widely available and smoked by many. At the same time, that weird thing killing people started acquiring names -GRID, and HTLV3, "gay cancer," the plague, then AIDS and ARC, and finally HIV.

Thatcher began to join me on weekly outings through the Bronx, distributing sterile injection equipment in those early, angry, grief fueled pre-legal days of syringe exchange. The difficulty of getting new sterile injecting equipment meant it was hard for us nascent syringe exchangers to get access to sufficient quantities of syringes to keep those we meet at our weekly site supplied with needles. Without these exchanges it meant most injectors resharpened the needles against the backs of matchbooks. These rigs were used until the needle broke, the plunger gave out or the unit numbers wore off – Sometimes, all at once.

I watched as heroin went from being sold from McDonald's coffee-stirrer sized spoons directly to your cookers or inside random folded slips of magazine paper, to plain glassine stamp collecting bags, then to glassine bags decorated with strips of colored tape ("get the red bag, it's the shit. Ha-ha"), then to glassine bags decorated with hand designed artwork using the same carved potato-and-ink stamp that children use to create holiday cards and individualized custom carved eraser-and-ink stamps, then to the pre-printed bags that can be purchased in bulk and selected from an on-line menu or purchased pre-printed from some bodegas today.

There are trends in the artwork: current films, current events, attempts at braggadocio, displays of prowess, cute animals, familiar consumer-culture logos, and puns. Generally heroin brands portray death, strength and trouble (Asesino). Cocaine brands tend to portray good living (Gucci). In this book you will see many of those. Our fears, our failures, our futures, our fantasies. That epidemic of the 80s never really left, but the mass dying ended in 1996 when antiretroviral medications turned AIDS, for those who could afford them, from a death sentence to a chronic disease. K2 smoking has supplanted crack and the idea of the "crack baby" has been debunked. New epidemics have since sailed in (HCV, then paused with effective oral medications, fentanyl-caused opiate overdose, a COVID19 pandemic, then made manageable with effective vaccines). Syringe exchange has been legal in NYC for almost 30 years now. Syringes can be purchased in many pharmacies without a prescription (look for the ESAP logo). Narcan distribution is common. Doctors prescribe Suboxone from their offices. There are many good resources for drug education, from how-to guides to rehab reviews. There's access to fentanyl test strips and drug testing vans to help solve the ever-persistent question bedeviling all who use non-pharmaceutical drugs --"what's in my bag". This past year NYC finally permitted safe consumption sites (or safe injection facilities, or overdose prevention centers) to open; the first two are run by the agencies where I work, with another planned and three to follow.

Some things have changed for the better. Some things could be better. Thatcher and I are still friends.
May you enjoy this abundance in good health.

-L. Synn Stern, RN, MPH

First edition 2023, Second printing 2025

Published by BLURRING BOOKS @BlurringBooksNYC

Editorial Assistance from Christopher Griffith and Sean M. Johnson

Number 4 in Blurring Books LSP series

Printed in the United Kingdom in a CarbonNeutral facility